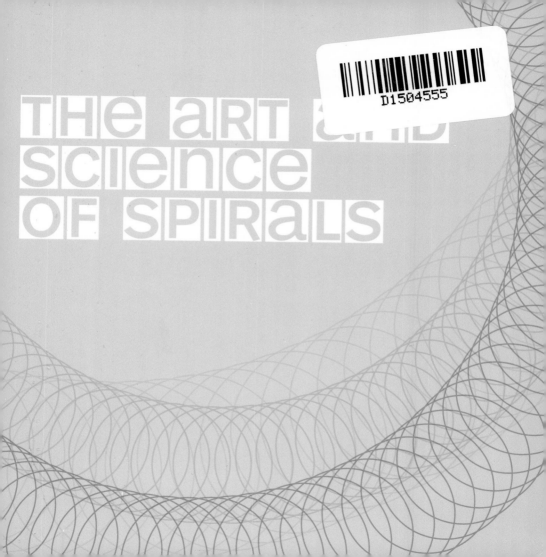

THE ART AND SCIENCE OF SPIRALS

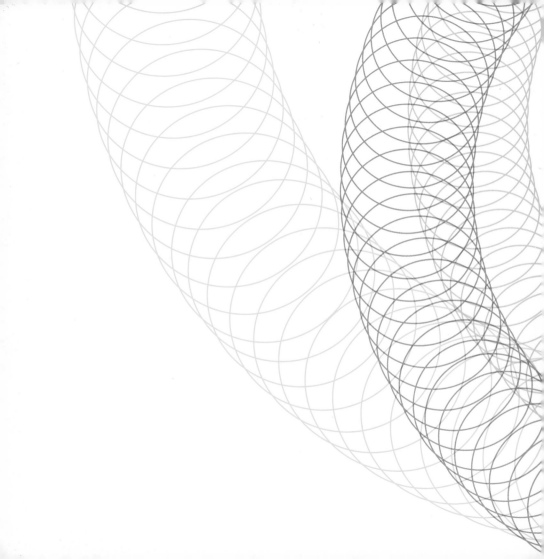

THE ART and Science OF SPIRALS

VICTOR DORFF

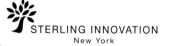

STERLING INNOVATION
New York

TO LISA SONNE,
WHOSE CREATIVITY,
INSIGHTS, SPIRIT, AND JOY
COMBINE TO MAKE HER
THE ORIGINAL
AND THE CONSUMMATE
POSSIBILITATOR.

STERLING INNOVATION and the distinctive Sterling Innovation logo are
registered trademarks of Sterling Publishing Co., Inc.

10

This 2009 edition published by Sterling Innovation.

Sterling Publishing Co., Inc.
387 Park Avenue South, New York, NY 10016

Cover and box design: Jo Obarowski
Interior design: Matthew Bouloutian and Vivian Ghazarian

Photography Credits
9: © Spacephotos.com/age fotostock
11: © 2005 Popular Science Magazine. All rights reserved. Reprinted from Popular Science
Magazine with permission of Bonnier Active Media, Inc.
12: © Artur Petrovsky (left); © Gaelic Wolf Consulting (right)
13: © Dave Hull (top); © Jonathan Lansey (bottom left); © Rosemarie Fiore (bottom right)

This book is part of *The Art and Science of Spirals* kit and is not to be sold separately.

Printed and bound in China

Sterling ISBN 978-1-4351-1582-8

contents

an INTRODUCTION 6
a HISTORICAL PERSPECTIVE 8
TRACING MOTION 10
GOING IN CIRCLES 14
THE "INSIDE" STORY 18
COUNTING TEETH 23
UNLOCKING THE MYSTERY OF FRACTIONS 27
MODULO NUMBERS 29
WHAT'S IN THE BOX? 31
PASCAL'S PAINKILLER 34
THE EQUATIONS 37
SAMPLE SPIRALS 42

an INTRODUCTION

RARELY DO THE SEPARATE WORLDS OF ART, MATHEMATICS, MECHANICS, AND CHILDREN'S TOYS CONVERGE AS WONDERFULLY AS THEY DO WITH THE SIMPLE DEVICE USED TO MAKE THIS FIGURE.

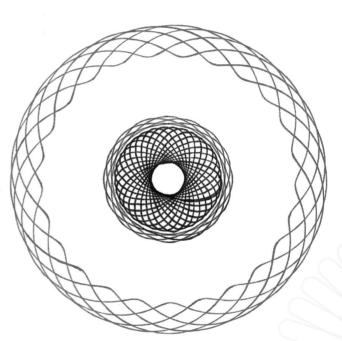

The apparatus consists of two wheels with meshing gear teeth. While pins are used to hold one wheel in place, the second wheel can be moved around the gear track on the stationary wheel using a pen inserted in a hole in the moving wheel. The pen traces the path taken as the wheel turns and moves forward simultaneously, creating the drawing.

The first such device was called a Spirograph. It was immensely popular when it came out forty years ago, and it continues to thrill and amaze people who discover it for themselves today.

At first, the fascination lies in being able to create such intricate designs by yourself. Then, as you become more comfortable making the drawings, you'll find yourself beginning to wonder, "Just how does this work?" At that moment, you will join some very prestigious company that has been fascinated by the mathematical principles behind such drawings, including such noted thinkers as Galileo, Pascal, and Descartes. They gave official-sounding names to each of the figures you are about to draw, and they recognized that those shapes contain some amazing properties that continue to be useful today.

Of course, you *could* spend a lifetime making spiral art without ever stopping to think about those men and their work, or about the math and science behind the pretty pictures. In fact, you probably *should* spend a little time playing with gears and making some artwork of your own before exploring the background of these fascinating figures.

But as you watch the wheels turn around and around, as you see the beauty take shape before your eyes and the questions begin to form in your mind, take a break and read about how it all got started. You may just find the entire process even more fascinating than you imagined.

a HISTORICAL PERSPECTIVE

INTERNET LEGEND HAS IT THAT THE SPIROGRAPH WAS INVENTED BY A NORTH ATLANTIC TREATY ORGANIZATION (NATO) WEAPONS ENGINEER IN THE SIXTIES, WHILE HE WAS WORKING TO DEVELOP A BOMB FUSE. THE TRUE STORY IS EVEN MORE INTERESTING.

Denys Fisher (1918–2002) had dropped out of college to join the family business in his native England, where his inventions increased the company's output of machine lubricants. In 1960, he began his own engineering firm, which quickly won a NATO weapons contract to produce tiny springs to exacting standards. Only then, with financial security in hand, was he able to focus on his real passion: a Victorian-era practice of using gears and cogs to draw intricate patterns. He spent Christmas of 1962 trying to develop a variety of such drawing tools, then gave up and put the project aside. Six months later, while listening to Beethoven's Ninth Symphony, he is said to have had a vision that led him to create the interlocking plastic pieces that children all over the world have been using ever since to make amazing patterns. Fisher's nested gears went from being an instant hit in England to a worldwide sensation when the U.S. toy company Kenner bought the rights. They called it a Spirograph, and it remains popular today.

The word "spirograph" has been used to describe many different devices. In the medical field, for example, the term refers to machines that measure breathing. In 1907, British inventor Theodore Brown called his disc-based moving-picture projecting system the spirograph. And as far back as the 1880s, Lithuanian mathematician Bruno Abdank-Abakanowicz called the drawing tool *he* invented a spirograph. Although the curves drawn with that tool are completely different from Denys Fisher's creation, many websites have confused the two and credit both men with the same invention.

Today, the Hasbro company owns a trademark on the word Spirograph, but "spirograph" has become synonymous in common usage with curves mathematicians call **EPITROCHOIDS** and **HYPOTROCHOIDS**. (We'll get to the math behind the art a little bit later.) It has even become the name of a cosmic cloud with a similar design. When astronomers saw pictures of this stellar formation sent back from the Hubble Space Telescope, they dubbed it the Spirograph Nebula. No matter what it's called, the beauty of the repeating spiral patterns captivates the eye, almost obscuring the simplicity of the design itself.

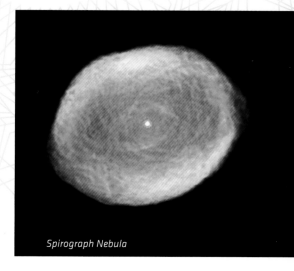

Spirograph Nebula

TRACING MOTION

THE DRAWING WE RECOGNIZE AS A SPIROGRAPH IS ACTUALLY CREATED BY TRACING THE PATH OF A MOVING OBJECT. ONE OF THE SIMPLEST WAYS TO CREATE SUCH PATTERNS IS BY USING A FREELY SWINGING PENDULUM.

About 100 years ago, it was quite popular to own a device called a harmonograph, which was constructed of a combination of pendulums that moved both the pen and the paper. The design of the drawing created by a **HARMONOGRAPH** would depend on the starting speed and direction of each pendulum *and* the degree to which the motion was "dampened"—that is, what friction was applied to each pendulum to bring it to a gradual stop.

One of the most interesting examples of a pendulum drawing is called the **EARTHQUAKE ROSE**. The sand-tracing pendulum was sitting in a shop when it was set into motion by an earthquake, and what it drew in the sand is a representation of the continued effect of the movement of the Earth and its aftermath. In today's electronic age, it has become possible to replace the sand and the physical swinging pendulum with an oscillating **LASER BEAM** glowing in the dark.

Pendulums "Draw" Novel Designs

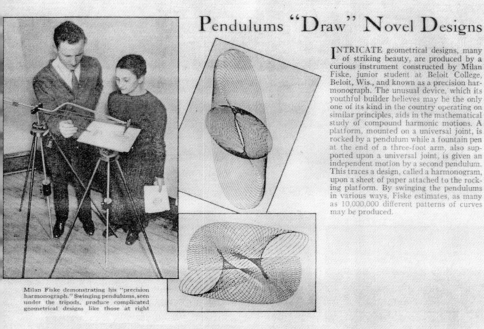

INTRICATE geometrical designs, many of striking beauty, are produced by a curious instrument constructed by Milan Fiske, junior student at Beloit College, Beloit, Wis., and known as a precision harmonograph. The unusual device, which its youthful builder believes may be the only one of its kind in the country operating on similar principles, aids in the mathematical study of compound harmonic motions. A platform, mounted on a universal joint, is rocked by a pendulum while a fountain pen at the end of a three-foot arm, also supported upon a universal joint, is given an independent motion by a second pendulum. This traces a design, called a harmonogram, upon a sheet of paper attached to the rocking platform. By swinging the pendulums in various ways, Fiske estimates, as many as 10,000,000 different patterns of curves may be produced.

Milan Fiske demonstrating his "precision harmonograph." Swinging pendulums, seen under the tripods, produce complicated geometrical designs like those at right

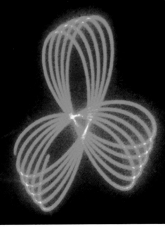

Laser beam

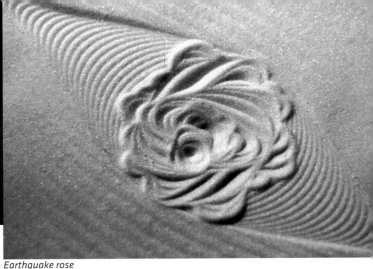
Earthquake rose

Some photographers have even risked their expensive cameras to create similar images by tossing them into the air, setting them spinning with the shutter open. The trick, of course, is to catch the camera *gently* before it hits the ground. While most photographers do *not* recommend this activity, those who *do* recommend it strongly suggest that it be tried over a mattress—at least the first few times.

Artists are using increasingly elaborate and creative approaches to designing art by tracing movement. One of the most interesting involved the use of a **CARNIVAL RIDE**. A giant spirograph-style image was made by using paint to trace the movement of the individual cars of this machine.

Denys Fisher's device for drawing spiral art seems much simpler, by comparison, but even the fundamental idea for a spirograph—tracing the motion of a point on a moving wheel—was quite a breakthrough when it was first discovered hundreds of years ago.

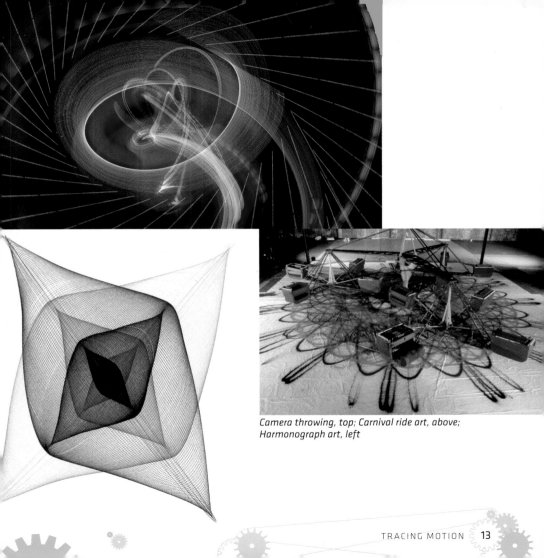

Camera throwing, top; Carnival ride art, above;
Harmonograph art, left

GOING
IN CIRCLES

IT'S EASY TO GUESS THAT, IF YOU PAINT A SPOT ON THE RIM OF A BICYCLE TIRE AND SPIN THE TIRE FREELY, THE SPOT WILL TRAVEL IN A CIRCLE. BUT IT'S A LITTLE HARDER TO IMAGINE WHAT HAPPENS TO THE PATH OF THE SPOT WHEN SOMEONE IS *RIDING* THE BIKE.

There's debate among historians over which fifteenth century mathematician noticed it first, but a point on a moving wheel follows its own unique curve. Galileo is credited with naming the path a "**CYCLOID**" at the end of the sixteenth century, and much of what we know about it today is the result of a mathematician's very painful toothache (but we'll get to that after we've had some more fun with the drawing).

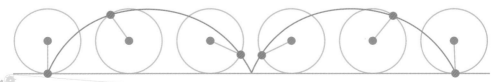

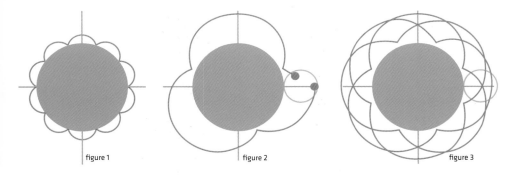

figure 1   figure 2   figure 3

First, let's have our imaginary bicyclist travel around the world, while we watch from a distance. The path of the point on the side of the tire, quite naturally, will be pretty circular. In the first figure, our cyclist had a bit of good luck because the drawing was complete after only one trip around the world, but it *could* happen differently.

Our cyclist might complete one "orbit," and find that the two ends of the curve don't match up, as seen in the second figure. To finish the drawing in the place where it began, our intrepid traveler will have to keep going. In this case, it takes three orbits before the spot on the tire begins to retrace its route. At that point, the path resembles the more ornate drawings we have come to think of as "spirographs," but which are officially called **EPICYCLOIDS**.

The factor that determines how many orbits will be required before the drawing is complete is the *ratio* of the size of the two circles. In order to figure out this ratio, let's start with two circles that are the same size. Quarters are a good prop, if you happen to have a couple handy.

Set the two quarters side by side, heads up, and put a little dot on each of them at the point where they touch. Before you start, see if you can predict what the path of the dot will look like. If you're really feeling adventurous, try to predict what position Washington's head will be in when the traveling quarter gets to the other side of the stationary one. (In fact, you may find this last exercise forms the basis for a pretty good bar bet, the next time the situation arises.) As you rotate one quarter around the other, note the path the dot takes, and how many revolutions the moving quarter

completes during its orbit. This vaguely heart-shaped version of an epicycloid is called, appropriately enough, a **CARDIOID**.

Notice that the moving quarter appears to make *two* full revolutions in the time it took to make one orbit around the stationary coin. Few people predict *that*.

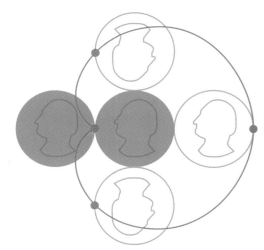

Doubling the size of the inner circle creates a curve called a **NEPHROID**, which means kidney-shaped. When the size ratio of the circles is increased to 3:1—meaning that the stationary circle is *three* times the size of the moving one—the drawing resembles a three-leaf clover.

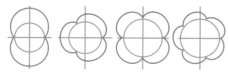

Clearly, a pattern is forming: as long as the size of one circle is a straight multiple of the other (i.e., the ratio is some whole number-to-one), we've learned that only one trip around the circle is required, and the number of petals will be the same as the ratio.

If the idea of trying to visualize watching a bicyclist pedal around the world seems a little too far-fetched, think bigger. Think about leaving the solar system and arriving at a point where you can watch as the planets travel around the sun. Now, picture the moon during the year, orbiting the Earth as it makes a giant circle. The path the moon takes is an epicycloid!

THE "INSIDE" STORY

THE PREFIX *epi-* REFERS TO THE FACT THAT EPICYCLOIDS ARE DRAWN ON THE *OUTSIDE* OF THE CIRCLE. OF COURSE, IT'S ALSO POSSIBLE FOR ONE CIRCLE TO ROLL ALONG THE *INSIDE* OF ANOTHER CIRCLE.

If we trace a point on a circle doing that, we get a curve called a **HYPOCYCLOID**. The simple hypocycloids resemble some of the basic figures you learned in elementary school, but with a significant difference.

When the ratio of the two diameters is 3:1 (meaning that the stationary circle *outside* is three times the size of the moving one *inside*), the hypocycloid looks like a triangle with inwardly curving sides. If you make

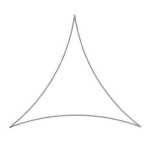

the small circle smaller—from *one-third* the diameter of the large circle to *one-quarter* of its size, or 4:1—the drawing changes to a four-pointed figure.

Change the ratio from 4:1 to 5:1, and the figure has five points, like a pentagon with sides curved inward.

By now, it should be fairly easy to predict the shape of the figure created when a circle travels around inside another that is ten times its size!

Just like their cousins the epicycloids, hypocycloids aren't always finished after the moving circle's first orbit. When that happens, the circle continues to orbit on its path until the two ends of the curve finally

meet. This five-pointed star is formed by the combination of a circle moving around the inside of another that is 2½ times its size. That means that, after one orbit, the inner circle will have completed 2½ revolutions, and the point that started adjacent to the outer ring will be on the other side of the circle.

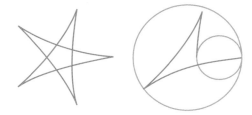

In such cases, although it is tempting to write the ratio as 2½:1, it is considered clearer to use only whole numbers in ratios. After one more orbit, the small circle is back at its starting position, and the drawing is complete. *Five* revolutions of the small circle send the mark on the wheel around the track *two* times, for a ratio of 5:2, which is the proper way to write the ratio of the sizes of the two circles.

At this point, you might have noticed that we skipped something. When we were talking about epicycloids, we began the conversation looking at circles of the same size, then one that was double the size of the other. Only then did we look at circles with a ratio of 3:1. Well, with hypocycloids, it's impossible for the two circles to be exactly the same size. If you tried to put a circle inside another that was the same size, it wouldn't work: the circles would be superimposed upon each other, and you'd wind up with only one.

An even stranger thing happens when you use an outer circle that is exactly double the size of the inner one. Care to guess what kind of path the mark on a tire would make as the cyclist rode around inside? A straight line! The logic of this is a little easier to see if you move the point off the rim and closer to the hub. Imagine, for example, the path of a reflector in the spokes of our bicycle tire. Even a small change brings a significant result: an oval.

By the way, moving the point off the rim does more than just change the shape. It also changes the mathematical *name* of the curves, from epi- and hypocycloids to epi- and hypo*trochoids*.

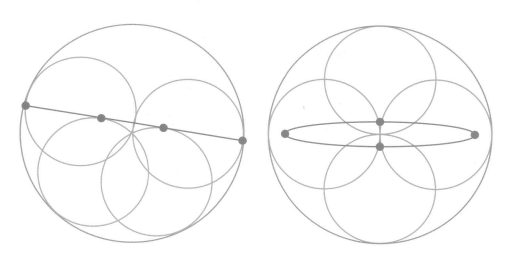

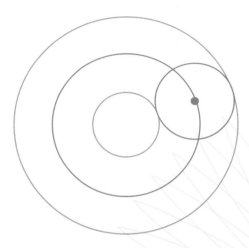

When you follow the path of the center of the circle as it makes its orbit, whether the moving circle is on the inside or the outside of the stationary one, no matter what size the circles are, the path formed by the center is another circle!

COUNTING TEETH

WE'VE ALREADY SEEN THAT IT'S THE RATIO OF THE SIZE OF THE TWO CIRCLES—THE STATIONARY ONE AND THE MOBILE ONE—THAT DETERMINES THE LEVEL OF INTRICACY IN THE DESIGN OF THE DRAWING.

With Denys Fisher's Spirograph, the circles are all designed as gears, and their sizes are measured in teeth. That means, to figure out what kind of drawing we're going to get from any combination of interlocking pieces, we need to know the **NUMBER OF TEETH** with which we'll be dealing. For some easy examples, let's begin with a stationary ring that has 100 teeth and try a variety of different-sized mobile gears. Keep in mind that, as the mobile gear travels around inside

the ring, it is matching its teeth with the ring's teeth, one at a time. The voyage is complete when the moving gear has made a whole number of revolutions *and* a whole number of orbits at *exactly* the same time. (Remember, the "orbit" refers to the path around the 100-toothed ring. The number of "revolutions" refers to how many times the moving gear spins through all of its teeth.)

Consider, first, a mobile gear with ten teeth. Once again, although the ratio of

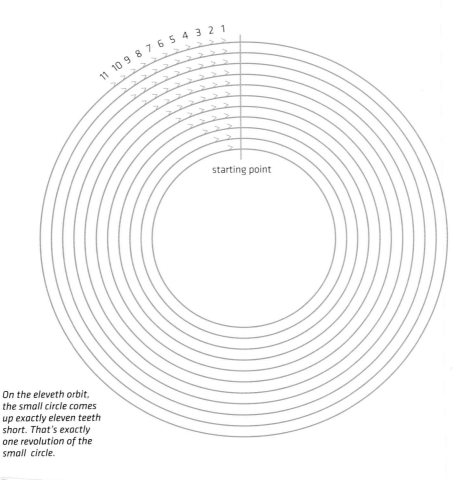

11 10 9 8 7 6 5 4 3 2 1

starting point

*On the eleveth orbit,
the small circle comes
up exactly eleven teeth
short. That's exactly
one revolution of the
small circle.*

circle sizes can be written as 100:10, it is considered clearer to write ratios with the smallest whole numbers that describe the same relationship. In this case, because both 100 and 10 can be divided by 10, the ratio is written as 10:1.

As the gear with ten teeth moves around inside the ring with 100, their teeth match up one by one. By the time the smaller circle has completed one revolution, its ten teeth have matched up with ten of the 100 teeth on the ring, and there are ninety to go.

By the time the moving circle completes its tenth revolution, it has traveled through "ten times ten" teeth. That is exactly the same number of teeth as on the stationary ring, so at that point the moving circle has completed exactly one orbit, and the ends of the curve meet in the same place.

Now, imagine that the moving gear has eleven teeth, while the stationary ring still has 100. That makes a ratio of 100:11. This ratio can't be reduced to a simple *some whole number*-to-one ratio, which is our first clue that the orbits and revolutions won't line up quite as easily.

Sure enough, after nine complete revolutions, the gear will have rotated past 99 teeth, and it will be one tooth short of a complete orbit. Another nine complete revolutions, and now it's *two* teeth short of its *second* complete orbit.

Around and around the small circle goes, and after each set of nine complete revolutions—passing ninety-nine teeth at a time—that little gear comes up one more tooth short of adding another orbit. After eleven sets of nine (ninety-nine) complete revolutions, the gear is exactly eleven teeth shy of finishing its eleventh orbit. Eleven teeth, however, is exactly one revolution of the small gear, so with one more revolution (to make 100), the gear has completed exactly eleven orbits. Once again, the **RATIO** of the gears (100:11) predicted how many revolutions and orbits it would take for the moving circle to wind up in exactly the same position as where it began its journey. So, a gear with ten teeth finished the job in one orbit. A gear with eleven teeth took eleven orbits. Care to guess how many orbits around a 100-toothed ring a gear with twelve teeth would need to end up exactly where it started?

Let's see what happens: Toward the end of the first orbit, the twelve-toothed gear has made eight complete revolutions and travelled across ninety-six teeth (12 x 8 = 96). That leaves it four teeth shy of a complete orbit. After the second round of eight revolutions, the twelve-toothed gear is now *eight* teeth short of two full orbits. After the third round of eight revolutions, it's twelve teeth short, which is the same as *one more revolution*. So at the end of three full orbits, the gear has made three rounds of eight revolutions, plus one more, for a total of twenty-five revolutions.

Notice that the ratio of 100:12 can be rewritten as 25:3, because both numbers are divisible by four.

There is some basic arithmetic at play here. With ten teeth, ten revolutions engage 100 teeth, or exactly the same as one orbit [10 • 10 = 100 • 1]. With eleven teeth, a gear needs eleven orbits to make 100 revolutions. The eleven orbits signify 1,100 teeth on the ring; the 100 revolutions signify 1,100 teeth on the gear [11 • 100 = 100 • 11]. So the first time an equal number of teeth have been engaged occurs at a ratio of 100 revolutions to eleven orbits.

With twelve teeth, a gear needs three orbits to make twenty-five revolutions. Both three orbits and twenty-five revolutions amount to 300 teeth. [12 • 25 = 100 • 3] And once again, the ratio of revolutions to orbits is the same as the ratio of the number of ring's teeth to the number of the gear's teeth—25:3.

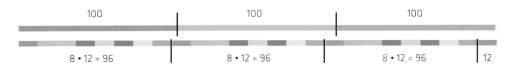

100	100	100	
8 • 12 = 96	8 • 12 = 96	8 • 12 = 96	12

UNLOCKING THE MYSTERY OF FRACTIONS

THE PROCESS OF PREDICTING THE NUMBER OF REVOLUTIONS AND ORBITS INVOLVED IN DRAWING SPIRALS USES THE SAME NUMERICAL TECHNIQUES NECESSARY TO ADD FRACTIONS TOGETHER.

When we found that 300 was the minimum number of teeth crossed between a twelve-toothed gear and a 100-toothed ring to complete a drawing, we discovered the least common multiple of 12 and 100. That's the same as finding the lowest common denominator, which would be the first step in adding, as an example, $1/12 + 1/100$.

Fractions are just another way of writing ratios. For example, 5:2 can be written as $5/2 = 2\frac{1}{2}$. Just like ratios, every fraction can be written more than one way.

We have already seen that 100:10 is the same as 10:1, because they both describe the same relationship of quantities. Similarly, we can rewrite fractions without changing their value by multiplying (or dividing) both the top and the bottom by the same number. For example, $1/2$ can be rewritten as

$$\frac{1 \cdot 2}{2 \cdot 2} = \frac{2}{4} \text{ or } \frac{1 \cdot 4}{2 \cdot 4} = \frac{4}{8}$$

without changing

the value of the number. This is important because we can only add two fractions if they have the same number on the bottom (called the **DENOMINATOR**). So, when trying to add fractions with different denominators, the trick is to find a multiple of both that you can use as a *common* denominator.

In our example, we want to rewrite $\frac{1}{12}$ and $\frac{1}{100}$ with the same denominator. The smallest number that is divisible by both 100 and 12 is 300—the same as the number of teeth that were crossed in the process of making an image with a ring of 100 teeth and a circle of twelve teeth. By using the reduced ratio we derived to compare 100 and 12, 25:3, we can rewrite $\frac{1}{12} + \frac{1}{100}$ as $(\frac{1}{12} \cdot \frac{25}{25}) + (\frac{1}{100} \cdot \frac{3}{3})$, or $\frac{25}{300} + \frac{3}{300}$. Then the two fractions are ready to be added together.

Wouldn't it have been a lot more fun learning about fractions in school if the teacher had started by bringing out this kit?

MODULO NUMBERS

THE CONTENTS OF THIS KIT ALSO PROVIDE an INTRODUCTION TO a MORE SOPHISTICATED BRANCH OF MATHEMATICS CALLED _MODULO_ NUMBERS— a WORLD WHERE 9 + 5 can EQUAL 2.

In fact, you are already somewhat familiar with the concept: If it's nine o'clock now, what time will it be in five hours? If you said, "Two o'clock," then you already know all about _mod_ twelve arithmetic.

Every twelve hours, the small hand of the clock is back in the same position, having made one full turn around the face of the clock. So to find out what time it is if we are adding a number larger than 12, ignoring a.m. and p.m., we don't really have to keep going around and around the clock.

For example, if it is nine o'clock and we want to know what time it will be in sixteen hours, we can ignore the first twelve hours, since we'll be right back where we started. _Then_, if we add the remaining four hours, we know it will be one o'clock.

The same would be true for twenty-eight hours, or forty hours. For the purpose of finding out what time it is on a twelve-hour clock, $4 = 16 = 28 = 40$. For the sake of clarity, we write this as $4_{\bmod 12} = 16_{\bmod 12} = 28_{\bmod 12} = 40_{\bmod 12}$.

What this really means is, for each of those numbers, dividing by twelve leaves a remainder of four. So if it is nine o'clock now, we can add $9 + 4$ and get thirteen, but $13_{\bmod 12} = 1_{\bmod 12}$, so we say that it will be one o'clock in four hours, in sixteen hours, in twenty-eight hours, and again in forty hours.

In the case of the matchup between a twelve-toothed gear and a 100-toothed ring, we can use the same kind of arithmetic to determine how many orbits will be required to complete the drawing. We know that $100 \div 12 = 8$ with a remainder of four, so we can say that $100 \bmod 12 = 4_{\bmod 12}$. That means that, when the twelve-toothed gear has completed one orbit, it will be four teeth off from the starting position.

What makes this kind of arithmetic useful is that we don't have to divide 200 by twelve to determine the remainder after two orbits. Since $100_{\bmod 12} = 4_{\bmod 12}$, we can quickly see that $200_{\bmod 12} = 8_{\bmod 12}$, which means that the twelve-toothed gear will be eight teeth off after two orbits.

After the third orbit, the total is 300 teeth, and since $100_{\bmod 12} = 4_{\bmod 12}$, $300_{\bmod 12} = 12_{\bmod 12}$. We can divide twelve by twelve and get a remainder of zero, so $12_{\bmod 12} = 0_{\bmod 12}$. That means the number of teeth engaged in three orbits is evenly divisible by twelve, and the twelve-toothed gear will be **EXACTLY** where it started!

WHAT'S IN THE BOX?

LOOKING AT THE GEARS THAT COME IN THE PACKAGE WITH THIS BOOK, WE CAN USE MODULAR ARITHMETIC TO FIGURE OUT HOW MANY TIMES AROUND THE RING EACH ONE HAS TO TRAVEL TO COMPLETE ITS DRAWING.

This kit comes with three **GEARS**, a two-sided **RING** (inside and outside), and a bar, which will allow you to make even more interesting designs. The smallest gear has thirty teeth, so we will need to do all our calculations with *mod* 30 arithmetic. Let's start with the inner ring, which has ninety-six teeth.

$96_{\mod 30} = 6_{\mod 30}$	After one orbit, the gear is off by six teeth.
$2(96_{\mod 30}) = 192_{\mod 30} = 12_{\mod 30}$	After two orbits, the gear is off by twelve teeth.
$3(96_{\mod 30}) = 288_{\mod 30} = 18_{\mod 30}$	After three orbits, the gear is off by eighteen teeth.
$4(96_{\mod 30}) = 384_{\mod 30} = 24_{\mod 30}$	After four orbits, the gear is off by twenty-four teeth.
$5(96_{\mod 30}) = 480_{\mod 30} = 0_{\mod 30}$	After five orbits, the match is perfect.

That means that five orbits are needed to complete the drawing when using the smallest gear and the inside ring.

Using modulo arithmetic throughout the problem can make things even easier. Notice that once we knew that one orbit was $6_{\mathrm{mod}\ 30}$, we could do *all* our arithmetic using six instead of ninety-six:

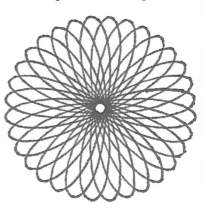

57-toothed gear, 96-toothed ring

$96_{\mathrm{mod}\ 30} = 6_{\mathrm{mod}\ 30}$	One orbit
$5(6_{\mathrm{mod}\ 30}) = 30_{\mathrm{mod}\ 30} = 0_{\mathrm{mod}\ 30}$	Five orbits

See if you can do your own modular arithmetic to calculate the requirements for drawing some of the other possible figures.

$96_{\mathrm{mod}\ 57} = \underline{\hspace{2cm}}_{\mathrm{mod}\ 57}$ After one orbit, the gear is off by $\underline{\hspace{1cm}}$ teeth.

$2(96_{\mathrm{mod}\ 57}) = \underline{\hspace{2cm}}_{\mathrm{mod}\ 57}$ After two orbits, the gear is off by $\underline{\hspace{1cm}}$ teeth.

$3(96_{\mathrm{mod}\ 57}) = \underline{\hspace{2cm}}_{\mathrm{mod}\ 57}$ After three orbits, the gear is off by $\underline{\hspace{1cm}}$ teeth.

$18(96_{\mathrm{mod}\ 57}) = 6 \cdot [3(96_{\mathrm{mod}\ 57})] = \underline{\hspace{2cm}}_{\mathrm{mod}\ 57}$ After eighteen orbits, the gear is off by $\underline{\hspace{1cm}}$ teeth.

$19(96_{\mathrm{mod}\ 57}) = 18(96_{\mathrm{mod}\ 57}) + 1(96_{\mathrm{mod}\ 57}) = \underline{\hspace{2cm}}_{\mathrm{mod}\ 57}$ After nineteen orbits, the gear is off by $\underline{\hspace{1cm}}$ teeth

75-toothed gear, 96-toothed ring

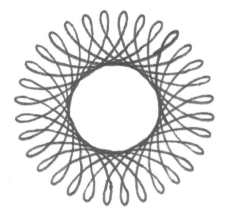

$96_{\text{mod } 75} =$ _____ $_{\text{mod } 75}$ After one orbit, the gear is off by _____ teeth.

$4(96_{\text{mod } 75}) =$ _____ $_{\text{mod } 75}$ After four orbits, the gear is off by _____ teeth.

$24(96_{\text{mod } 75}) = 6 \cdot [4(96_{\text{mod } 75})] =$ _____ $_{\text{mod } 75}$ After twenty-four orbits,

the gear is off by _____ teeth.

$25(96_{\text{mod } 75}) = 24(96_{\text{mod } 75}) + 1(96_{\text{mod } 75}) =$ _____ $_{\text{mod } 75}$ After twenty-five orbits,

the gear is off by _____ teeth.

PASCAL'S PAINKILLER

THE EARLY PART OF THE SEVENTEENTH CENTURY WAS A GOLDEN AGE OF SCIENCE. SOME OF THE MOST FAMOUS SCIENTISTS AND MATHEMATICIANS OF ALL TIME LIVED DURING THAT PERIOD.

Galileo, who gave the name cycloid to the curved path of a point on the rim of a wheel, was one of the foremost pioneers of that era. Of course, he is far better known as the scientist who invented the refracting telescope, and who discovered that objects fall at the same speed, regardless of their mass. But he spent a lot of time exploring the characteristics of the shape he had named.

When Galileo focused his insatiable curiosity on the cycloid, one of the first things he wanted to figure out was the area under a single arch of a cycloid curve. Galileo tried, and failed, to find the answer using traditional mathematical tools. Then he began cutting and weighing pieces of metal in the shape of the curve to **ESTIMATE** the area. Comparing the weights, Galileo declared that the area was approximately three times larger than the area of the circle used to create the curve.

In 1634, mathematician G.P. de Roberval proved that the area of a cycloid was, in fact, **EXACTLY** three times that of its generating circle. Twenty-four years later, in 1658, Christopher Wren (now more famous for his architecture than his math) showed that the length of a cycloid was four times the diameter of the generating circle.

It was common practice for mathematicians of that time to pose problems to one another, announcing that they had already found the solution and challenging colleagues to do the same. The cycloid proved such fertile ground for those contests, generating some very heated debates, that it is often referred to as the "Helen of Geometers."

Blaise Pascal was one of the most creative mathematicians of that era. He was a child prodigy who showed great promise in geometry, and as an adult his work led to the development of probability theory. In 1654, after surviving an accident that nearly took his life, Pascal gave up mathematics to dedicate his life to Christianity. Nevertheless, when he was lying in bed with a terrible toothache in 1658, Pascal tried to distract himself with thoughts of the cycloid curve. As he fell deeper into thought, the pain seemed to ease, and Pascal saw this as a sign from God that he should continue his mathematical exploration of this class of curves.

As a result of that bout with dental pain, Pascal solved several problems related to the cycloid: the area under any segment of the cycloid, the center of gravity of a segment, and the volume and surface area of the egg-shaped solid formed by rotating the cycloid around its base in three dimensions. Then, as was typical of his time, Pascal issued a challenge to the rest of the world to solve the problems he had just solved.

At about the same time, others began to make some amazing discoveries about the curve's physical properties: turning the cycloid curve upside down turns it into a remarkable ramp.

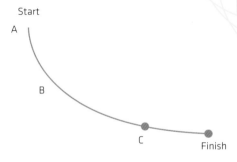

Start

A

B

C

Finish

In 1657, Christian Huygens invented the pendulum clock, and had become interested in the way gravity affected freely falling objects. What he noticed about the cycloid curve was that, regardless of where an object was placed on the ramp, it took the same length of time to reach the bottom. A curve with this characteristic is called a **TAUTOCHRONE**.

It wasn't until 1690 that Jakob Bernoulli was able to prove, mathematically, that the cycloid was the tautochrone. Six years later, Jakob's brother Johann proved that the cycloid was also the **BRACHISTOCHRONE**, the shape of a slope that creates the fastest path for an object traveling from top to bottom.

In the course of making these discoveries, these mathematicians used some of the techniques that would later evolve into what we today call calculus, and they were laying the groundwork for the design of some of the most exciting roller coasters *ever*.

THE EQUATIONS

COMPUTER ANIMATION HAS BECOME SO COMMON-
PLACE, MOST OF US DON'T GIVE IT A SECOND THOUGHT.
FRENCH PHILOSOPHER AND MATHEMATICIAN
RENE DESCARTES (OF "I THINK, THEREFORE I AM"
FAME) DESERVES CREDIT FOR MAKING IT POSSIBLE.

Back in the seventeenth century, when cycloids were all the rage, Descartes came up with a way to express geometric shapes as the kinds of algebraic equations used in programming computers today.

To get an idea of how it works, think of all the pairs of numbers you can add together to get "4" as the answer. How many pairs did you think of? You probably began with these: "0 and 4," "1 and 3," "2 and 2." Of course,

after a moment, you may have thought to include "3 and 1," and "4 and 0." That's when most people get stuck. If you also consider fractions (e.g., "½ and 3½") and negative numbers (e.g., "5 and –1"), however, the list of solutions becomes (literally) endless.

Although there is no way to make a complete list of all the number pairs that add up to "4," Descartes provided a way to draw a picture of the results. He proposed creating a two-dimensional graph by, essentially, putting two rulers together at a 90-degree angle to create a grid.

Descartes suggested labeling each point on the grid with one number to indicate its horizontal position, and another number to represent its vertical position. When each of the five whole-number pairs above is represented as a dot on the grid, it is easy to see that the collection forms a straight line. Perhaps even more remarkable is that the two coordinates of any point along that line will add up to "4."

What this means is, this drawing, which geometry refers to generally as a "line," can also properly be referred to as the solution to the algebraic equation $x + y = 4$, and every geometric "point" can also be thought of as an ordered pair of numbers, (x, y).

The curves that can be drawn with the interlocking gears can also be represented with equations, but they are somewhat more complicated than the one that forms a line. To understand them, we need to make a quick detour into another one of the intersections between algebra and geometry: **TRIGONOMETRY**.

As complicated as trigonometry looks when it is written out on paper, the idea is very simple: triangles that have the same shape have proportional sides.

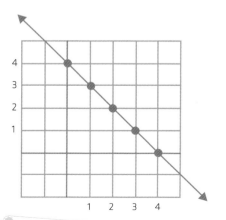

In other words, the lengths of each of the corresponding pairs of sides on these two triangles form the same ratio.

Let's name each of the sides: there's the side *opposite* (*O*) the angle, the side *adjacent* (*A*) to the angle, and the side called the *hypotenuse* (*H*).

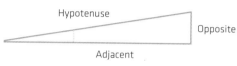

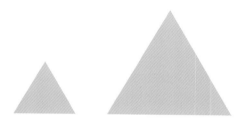

Those ratios provide a way to express an angle as a number. Consider that any angle we draw can be turned into a triangle by dropping a line straight down between the two legs, at any point we choose. All the different triangles have the same shape, and no matter what size triangle we create from the angle in this manner, the proportions between any two of its sides are always the same.

From those three sides, we can identify six different proportions, but only two become involved in the equation for our drawings: *O/H* is called the *sine* of an angle, and *A/H* is called the *cosine*.

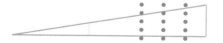

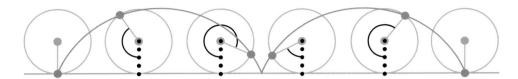

Take a look, one last time, at the way a simple cycloid is formed. For simplicity, let's assume the radius of the circle making our cycloid is "1." (The radius of a circle is the distance from its center to any point *on* the circle.)

At any moment, as the circle moves, two imaginary lines form an angle we can measure: the line from the center straight down to the "ground," and the line from the center to the point on the rim. In a way, the size of that angle represents how much the circle has moved from its initial position. Let's call it "*t*."

If we use Descartes' method for turning a drawing into an equation, all we have to do is identify the location of the points of the curve we are drawing relative to the two rulers that make up the coordinate grid. Here's how we do it in the case of a cycloid: for the horizontal distance from the starting point, we can measure it as [$x = t - \sin(t)$], and the vertical distance is determined by [$y = 1 - \cos(t)$].

$x = t - \sin(t)$

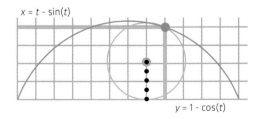

$y = 1 - \cos(t)$

Equations of that form, where the horizontal and vertical positions are identified separately relative to some third measurement, are called **PARAMETRIC EQUATIONS**. If you prefer the more familiar form of an equation, here is what the one for cycloids looks like (with a representing the measurement of the radius of the moving circle):

$$x = a \cos^{-1}\left(1 - \frac{y}{a}\right) - \sqrt{2ay - y^2}$$

(By the way, if you have read this far, you are entitled to a little recognition from your friends and family. After you have finished drawing your next spiral masterpiece, scribble that formula next to it. If anyone asks, just shrug modestly and smile.)

Sample Spirals

WE CAN ALL BE THANKFUL TO DENYS FISHER FOR INVENTING A SIMPLE TOOL THAT MAKES DRAWING THESE AMAZING FIGURES EASY ENOUGH FOR A CHILD TO DO (AND AN ADULT, TOO)! NOW IT'S YOUR TURN.

The cycloid provides more than enough to think about, but the fun really starts when you begin to draw your own.

Using interlocking gears and some different colored pens, you can make your own art from the curves that fascinated a generation of history's greatest minds.

For best results, use pushpins to secure the rod and circle templates (or even another gear) to corrugated cardboard. Here are some to get you started. Count the holes from the end (not the center) of the gear, insert a pen, and turn it around the inside of the circle template (unless otherwise indicated) or the outside of the rod. Create and combine figures to form your own magnificent designs!

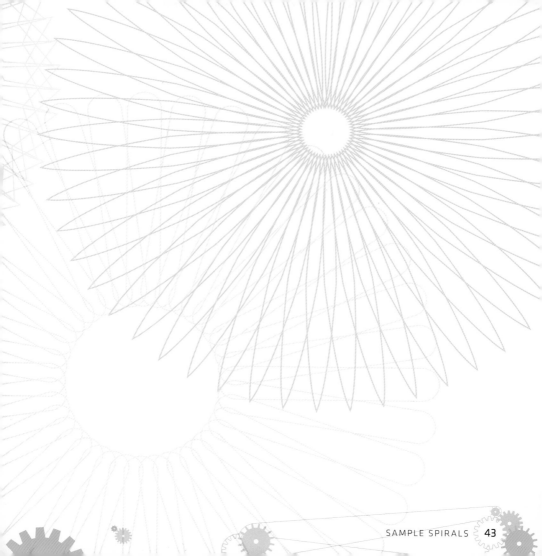

Small gear, hole 8
Medium gear, hole 12

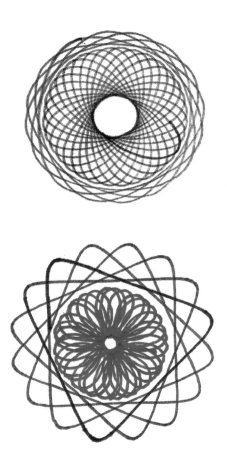

Large gear, hole 18
Small gear, hole 3

Large gear, hole 3

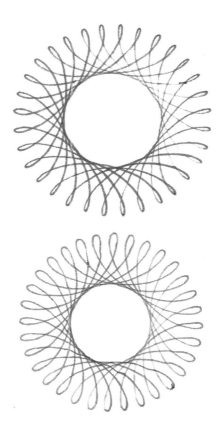

Large gear, hole 4

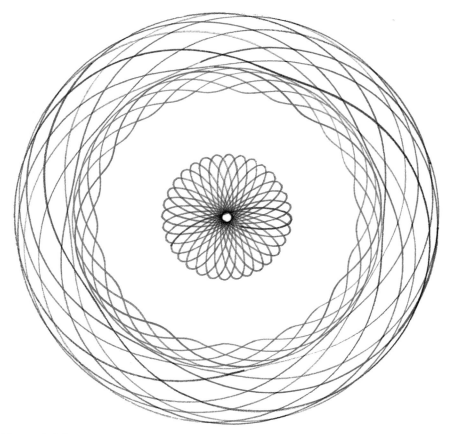

Middle gear, hole 8
Small gear, hole 6 (outside of template)
Large gear, hole 17 (outside of template), using three different colors

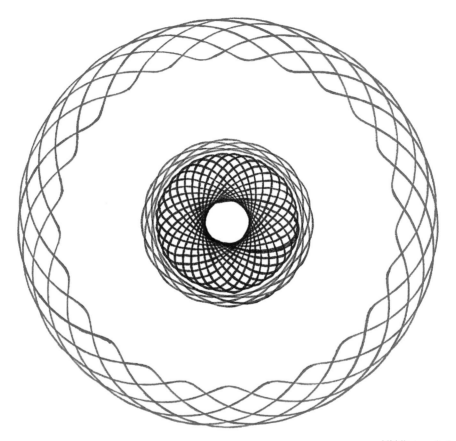

Middle gear, hole 12
Small gear, last hole
Small gear, hole 1 (outside of template)

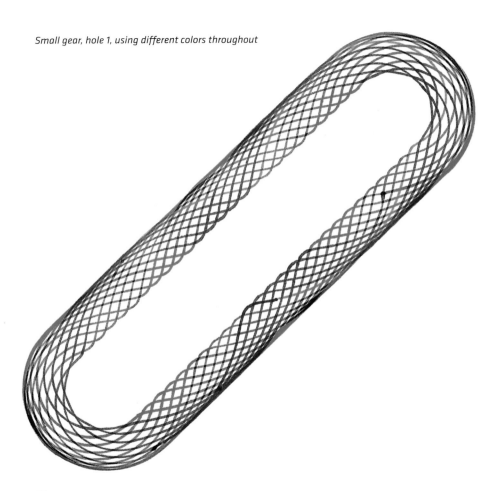

Small gear, hole 1, using different colors throughout

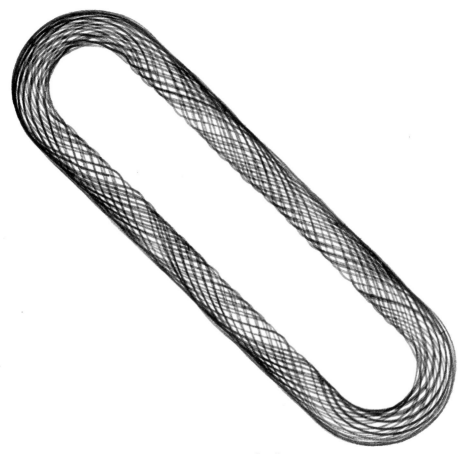

Small gear, hole 5, using different colors throughout

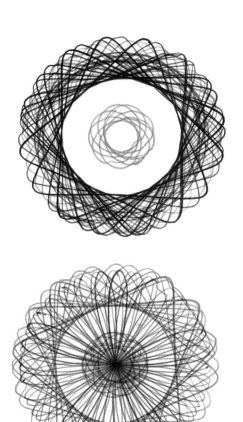

Small gear, hole 1
Small gear, last hole
Small gear, hole 5
Large gear, last hole

Middle gear, hole 2
Large gear, hole 1
Small gear, hole 1

Small gear, hole 7
Medium gear, hole 5

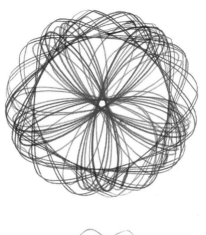

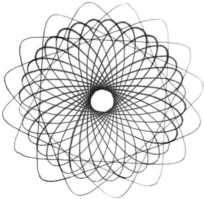

Middle gear, hole 10
Small gear, hole 2

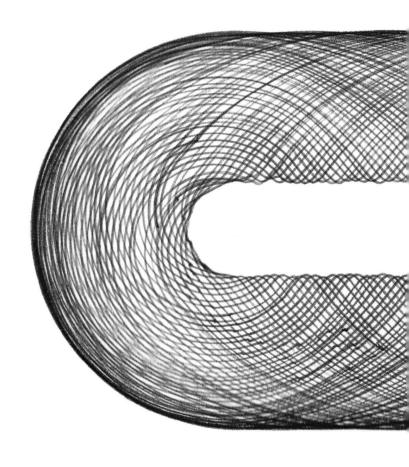

Large gear, hole 1

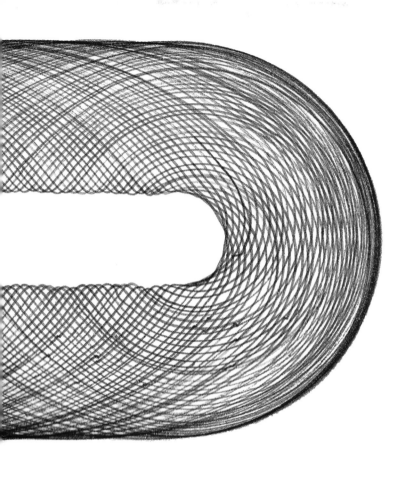

Medium gear, hole 16
Medium gear, hole 15
Small gear, hole 6

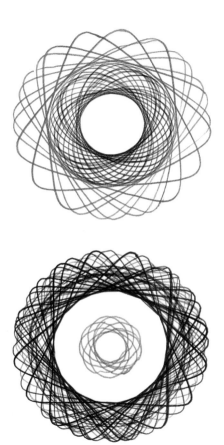

Small gear, hole 1
Small gear, last hole
Small gear, hole 5
Large gear, last hole

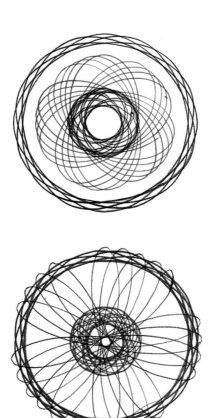

Medium gear, hole 13
Small gear, last hole
Large gear, last hole

Medium gear, hole 5
Large gear, last hole
Small gear, last hole

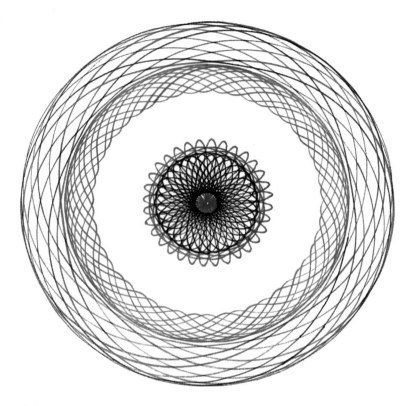

Middle gear, hole 1
Middle gear, hole 11
Small gear, last hole
Small gear, hole 1 (outside of template)
Large gear, hole 18 (outside of template), using different colors throughout